W9-CLC-727

Praise for the
Caught Up in Love Series

Caught Up in RAINE (Book #1)
2017 IPPY AWARD-WINNER (Bronze) in Romance

"O'Connor's contemporary romance is very realistic and will tug on the heartstrings of probably more readers than she expected … Jillian and Raine have faced a lifetime's worth of secrets and heartbreaks … you'll want to cheer them on until the very end." ~*RT Book Reviews*

"The plot is driven by a May-December premise that is blown away in the sexy love scenes." ~*Library Journal*

"For all the contemporary romance fans out there, this book is for you." ~*Night Owl Reviews*

"Urban fantasy author O'Connor (Trinity Stones) branches out into romantic women's fiction with a sexy tale of angst, guilt, love, and hate." ~*Publishers Weekly*

"LG O'Connor had me at "hello" with this plot…a hard to beat Romance for 2016…" ~*HEA Romances with a Little Kick Blog*

"This story is both beautiful and haunting... I loved every second of this sexy, sweet and romantic book!!!" ~*The Romance Reviews, Top Pick, 5 stars*

"Caught Up in Raine brought me to laughter and to tears. O'Connor's characters are complex, with strengths, fears, insecurities, and a depth of emotion that bring them to vibrant life on the page." ~*The Romance Dish*

"O'Connor delivers a unique women's fiction story packed with emotion, humor and sexiness. I could not turn the pages quickly enough..." ~**Caridad Pineiro,** *NY Times &* *USA Today* **Bestselling Romance Author**

"WOW! What an absolutely fantastic story! I absolutely fell in love with Raine, and wanted Jillian for a girlfriend! Well written and very relevant as a contemporary romance with two amazing, memorable characters." ~***Carla Susan Smith, Author of A Vampire's Promise***

Rediscovering Raine (Book #1.1)

"The writing is gorgeous; it's a beautifully touching story that warms the heart and gives you hope. I am truly in awe of Ms. O'Connor who could make me feel so much in just a few pages." ~***Book Obsessed Chicks Book Club***

"Proving herself a force to be reckoned with in the world of contemporary romance, L.G. O'Connor does not disappoint with this addition to her series." ~***Amazon Review***

Caught Up in Rachel (Book #1.2)

"If *Caught Up In Raine* is the cake, and *Rediscovering Raine* the frosting, then *Caught Up In Rachel* is the decoration on top. L.G. O'Connor has once again proved herself an exceptional story-teller, able to capture all the fear and wonderment of becoming a new parent with this welcome addition to her series. A remarkable gift for inviting her readers to experience all the joys and heartache of her characters, I can hardly wait to see what she has in store for future novels." *~Amazon Review*

"A beautiful and inspiring story full of tender moments." *~Love at 1st Read*

Shelter My Heart (Book #2)

"A well polished, wonderfully written love story driven by believable characters whose strengths and flaws add complexity to a fairy-tale romance." *~IndieReader, 4.5 stars*

Caught Up in Love Series
Three Women. One Story.

The Caught Up in Love series centers around three New Jersey women: romance writer Jillian Grant; her sister, Katherine "Kitty" McNally Lynch; and Kitty's daughter, Jenny Lynch. They are all part of a family plagued by loss. Each woman harbors her own guilty secret and must journey through her personal pain to find redemption and ultimately surrender her heart for a second chance to get caught up in love.

Jillian & Raine's Story
Caught Up in RAINE (Book #1)
Rediscovering Raine (Book #1.1)
Caught Up in Rachel (Book #1.2)

Jenny & Devon's Story
Shelter My Heart (Book #2)
One Summer Day (Prequel Novelette)

COMING SOON

Kitty & John's Story
Surrender My Heart (Book #3)

Caught Up in Christmas (A novella) COMING 2018
Join Jillian, Kitty, Jenny, and their families for one last tale, and the bittersweet conclusion to the Caught Up in Love series.

Sign up for the CAUGHT UP IN LOVE NEWSLETTER at www.lgoconnor.com for release updates and extras!

L G O'CONNOR

Recipes From Raine's Roost aka Jillian's Kitchen

BY RAINE MACDONALD

First Seen on USA Today Happy Ever After

Copyright 2016 L.G. O'Connor
Published by Collins-Young Publishing LLC

License Notes

Recipes originally appeared between December 2015 and December 2016 as blog posts on USA Today Happy Ever After blog. They remain the intellectual property of L.G. O'Connor. The character, Raine MacDonald, is wholly owned by, and the intellectual property of, L.G. O'Connor. Photo Credits: L.G. O'Connor. Author Photo Credit: Kimberly Rocha.

All rights reserved. No part of this publication may be reproduced, distributed, or transmitted in any form or by any means, including photocopying, recording, digital scanning, or other electronic or mechanical methods, without the prior written permission of the publisher, except in the case of brief quotations embodied in critical reviews and certain other noncommercial uses permitted by copyright law.

For permission requests, please address Collins-Young Publishing, LLC, 1 Sentry Lane #6, Chester, NJ 07930

Published 2017
ISBN: 978-0-9970623-7-3 (Trade Paperback)

This is a work of fiction. Names, characters, places, and incidents portrayed in this novel are either products of the author's imagination or are used fictitiously, and any resemblance to actual persons, living or dead, business establishments, events, or locales is entirely coincidental.

Sign up for the CAUGHT UP IN LOVE NEWSLETTER for special updates.

Contents

Praise for the Caught Up in Love Series   i

Foreword   xi

Sweet Potato and Banana Puree   1

Mac-a-Tastic Mac 'n Cheese   5

Bonus: Mini-Meatloaf—Raine Style   11

Chocolate-covered Strawberries   13

Chicken Tortilla Soup & Easy Guac   17

Cheddar & Bacon Egg Strata   23

Glazed Salmon, meal-in-a-pan   28

Shrimp & Orzo   33

Crab Deviled Eggs—à la Raine   38

Yellow Watermelon & Tomato Salad with Lime & Honey Vinaigrette   42

Herb & Heirloom Tomato Tart   49

Rosemary-Lemon Chicken Thighs   54

Chestnut, Apple and Sausage Stuffing, Raine-style   58

Not-so-green Holly Cookies   64

Note to the Readers   69

Want more?   71

About the Author   81

Other Books   82

Foreword

Get caught up in love with Jillian & Raine

"Haunting and beautiful." "Sweet, sexy, and romantic!" *The Romance Reviews, Top Pick*

Food = Love

It's a simple enough equation, isn't it? You may wonder what food has to do with romance, but to me, a hero who's willing to cook for the heroine tells me something essential about his heart. I feel privileged that Raine MacDonald came into my life along with the rest of the *Caught Up in Love* cast. I adore him, and I hope you will, too!

That said, I'm continually amazed, humbled, and grateful for the opportunities I've received as an author. Some even make me chuckle. Like the one that made this cookbook possible. For anyone who knows me personally, they can appreciate the irony of this publication, which is a compilation of my hero, Raine's year-long recipe column on the **USA *Today's* Happy Ever After** blog. A ton of thanks goes to my publicist, Kim Miller, for securing Raine the gig, and to Joyce Lamb for allowing him to take over her column once a month for a baker's dozen worth of posts between December 2015 and December 2016. My unending gratitude goes to both of them for believing in him and giving us both the chance to share *Recipes from Raine's Roost.*

The ironic part of this story is that while Raine knows how to finesse his way around a kitchen, I'm more like my heroine, Jillian. I rather clean a toilet than cook. It's not that I can't cook, I just don't particularly enjoy it. Don't get me wrong, I love good food and have a special appreciation for a hot guy wearing an apron. To quote Jillian, "I'm in the business of selling women's fantasies," and there's something to be said for a sexy man who knows the difference between a saucepan and a skillet. Jillian's a romance novelist, like me, who has never embraced her inner Julia Child and is happy getting by on whatever she can scrape together: a cup of yogurt, cereal, chocolate…you get the picture. This causes some angst for Jillian's older sister Kitty, who hosts Sunday dinners to ensure Jillian eats at least one decent meal a week. Jillian's no fool. When Raine offers to play chef to repay her for giving him a place to stay, she readily jumps at the exchange, and soon food isn't the only thing sizzling in the kitchen!

My aversion to cooking aside, I can knock a recipe out of the park when I put my mind to it. The easier, the better. After Raine's maiden post landed him the column, my husband laughed and said, "Well, at least I'll get twelve home-cooked meals this year!" Ha! The little joker… I'm lucky he didn't marry me for my nightly delivery of culinary delights.

All of Raine's recipes are from my list of personal favorites. They are tried and true and have all been adapted and presented with Raine's spin. If known, I've listed original sources. Many are simple enough that you can find many variations on the Internet. What makes these posts uniquely Raine's are his anecdotes, stories, and his interpretation of ingredients and prep instructions. More than sharing his recipes, Raine gives you a glimpse of himself and Jillian, their relationship, and their life together. Raine appreciates readers as much as I do. He has his own Twitter handle (@ Raines_Roost) if you want to stay in touch!

At the end of this cookbook, I've included an exclusive excerpt of *Caught Up in RAINE* that's not available unless you purchase the book. I've also added a mini meatloaf bonus recipe that only my newsletter subscribers have received. CUIR is the first in the *Caught Up in Love* series, about three women in the same family: Jillian, her niece Jenny, and her sister Kitty. All of whom make an appearance in these pages. The series theme: "Sometimes you must confront ghosts of the past for a second chance at love." Each woman has a guilty secret and must travel her own personal road to redemption. This family-based series is written as standalone novels with recurring characters and a unifying thread that pulls everything together in the end but doesn't interfere with the individual stories. Themes of love, death, hope, and honor run deep throughout the series, but don't weight it down, making this a romantic women's fiction hybrid with the heat of romance and the depth of women's fiction.

In closing, a big shout-out goes to my BFF, Stacey Caron, food blogger extraordinaire, who blogs under Stacey Snacks Online. She taught me everything I know about cooking back in our "Club Zero" days. Because of her, I actually do know the difference between a saucepan and a skillet. Check her out on Instagram and here:

www.staceysnacksonline.com

To stay in touch and for new release updates and extras, consider signing up for the CAUGHT UP IN LOVE NEWSLETTER .

Happy Cooking!

L.G. O'Connor

Sweet Potato and Banana Puree

This post originally appeared December 17, 2015 on
the *USA Today* **Happy Ever After** Blog.

RAINE

Hey. How's it going? Welcome to my first post. For the record, this was Jillian's idea. She thought I should share my mad cooking skills with the world. Well, maybe not the whole world, but people like me who have partners with an aversion to kitchens. We can't let them starve, can we?

For those of you who don't know me, when I first met Jillian all she had in her fridge was a jug of water, a jar of mustard and a half loaf of bread. Her freezer was empty except for an old bag of ice. I thought, *Damn, what does this woman eat?* I'm the only thing standing between real food and Jillian living on take-out and Lean Cuisines.

That said, for someone with a hate-hate relationship with her kitchen, she's a wicked sous-chef. She kept me from losing my mind our first Thanksgiving together when I decided to cook for her family and make everything from scratch. Not sure what the hell I was thinking. Anyway, I digress. She thought I should offer up her favorite recipe from that near disaster in time for the holidays. Her sister Kitty asked me to make it this year for Christmas. So here goes...

SWEET POTATO AND BANANA PUREE
—RAINE STYLE

- 6 Big Sweet Potatoes (Get the ones with really orange skins. The light skin ones? Disastrous.)
- 2 decent-sized Bananas
- ½ cup of Maple Syrup (Use the pure stuff; don't cheap out.)
- 2 Tablespoons Ground Cinnamon
- 2 teaspoons Pumpkin Pie Spice (Who knew this stuff even existed?)
- ½ teaspoon Salt (Kosher, step away from the fancy Pink Himalayan...)

- Container of Candied Pecans (I get mine from Whole Foods.)

Preheat oven to 425 F. Stab the sweet potatoes with a fork and bake them until that fork sinks into the potatoes like a knife through soft butter—about 1 hour. But set the timer for 45 minutes then throw in the bananas—skins and all— with the potatoes on the baking sheet. Keep everything going for another 15 minutes, and then take the baking sheet out of the oven.

Let the potatoes and bananas cool for a few minutes until they can be handled, and then peel everything.

Remember I told you not to buy the light skin sweet potatoes, but go for the darker skin ones? Why? Because they're easier to puree. The first year I made this to bring to my friend Mikey's (pre–Jillian), I burned out my damn blender. Total freaking disaster. That was my first mistake; my second was using a blender and not a food processor. Lesson learned. Still, I usually puree in 2-3 batches. I just split the maple syrup, dry ingredients, and potatoes/bananas into twos or threes, puree, and then transfer to a 9-inch square baking dish. Then I make it look nice by smoothing out the top with a rubber spatula.

When that's all done, I garnish with the candied pecans in a cool zigzag pattern.

Bake at 300 degrees until it's heated through—usually about

20 minutes. Sometimes I make this the night before, since it takes a while to prep. I highly recommend enlisting a hot sous-chef to help. Worked like a charm for me.

That's it! It tastes amazing. Big time. Problem is, once someone gets a taste, they ask you to bring it for the next big occasion. Yup. At least that's what Kitty did to me…

If you end up making this, drop me a line and let me know how it turned out. Trust me, you can't go wrong. I eat it for dessert until it's gone. It's that good—for real.

Take it easy until next time.
—Raine

Mac-a-Tastic Mac 'n Cheese

This post originally appeared January 14, 2016 on the *USA TODAY* **Happy Ever After** Blog.

RAINE

Hey. How's it going? I'm stoked to be here, and I want to thank Joyce Lamb for inviting me back. I'll admit, when Jillian first talked me into doing this, I thought: *Who's going to want recipes from some half-naked guy with long hair?* So, thanks to everyone who shared my post and commented on social media. I'm touched by all the support. Really.

Remember I told you guys that Kitty asked me to bring it for Christmas? Needless to say, there wasn't any left for dessert the next day.

So on to this month's recipe ...

Let me start by explaining the title so you don't think I'm nuts. I grew up next door to a guy named Mikey Petrillo. Without getting into any history, he's been my best friend since high school and nicknamed me "Mac." Not a stretch when your last name is MacDonald. But he didn't stop there. Mikey created a whole Mac-abulary that he uses whenever

I'm around, though he usually reserves it for more salacious purposes.

Of course I told Jillian, so that's how she describes my home-made mac and cheese: Mac-a-Tastic. The first time I made it for her, she'd been jamming on a writing deadline and was stressed out beyond belief. If I hadn't intervened, she would've lived on a steady diet of coffee and dry toast … and maybe yogurt. And chocolate. Definitely chocolate.

One more piece of useless trivia for the curious, since I've gotten some questions about "Raine's Roost," and then we'll roll. Promise. Any guesses? Nope, we don't raise chickens. Any more guesses? No? OK, I'll tell you. Jillian had a sign made for my birthday and hung it over the stove. According to her, she always seems to find me in the kitchen when she, well, can't find me. The kitchen. It's where I roost. According to her.

So here we go … If you have a sexy sous-chef, grab him or her, and let's get started.

I adapted this recipe from David Page of Home Restaurant on Cornelia Street in NYC's West Village. If you ever get a chance to go there, have the original recipe. It's freaking amazing, but it's nothing like mine. When I say adapted, I mean I changed the recipe beyond recognition. If you looked at them side-by-side, they barely look like cousins. I'll point out some of the changes as we go. The first difference—he bakes his in an iron skillet

MAC-A-TASTIC MACARONI AND CHEESE

- 4 Tablespoons unsalted butter
- 1 large onion, diced (My onion dicer just died. Since I hate crying when I cook, I pick up a container of fresh diced organic onions in the produce aisle at Kings. Oh, and don't use the whole thing. ¼ container = approx. 1 onion)
- 1 Tablespoon minced garlic
- 3 Tablespoons flour (The first time I made this, I had to duck out and buy a new bag—Jillian's flour had expired in 2005. Who keeps flour that long?)
- 2½ cups 2% milk (The original recipe calls for 4 cups of whole milk. I cut it down and use 2% to save on the fat. It also makes the recipe less gooey—that should be a technical term.)
- 1 teaspoon paprika
- ½ teaspoon ground nutmeg (I grate the nuts myself. Try not to grate your fingers. You know what I'm sayin'.)

- 2 teaspoons kosher salt
- 1 teaspoon freshly ground black pepper (I usually premix the paprika, nutmeg, salt and pepper in a small soufflé dish)
- ¾ cup grated smoked Gouda (Original recipe uses extra-sharp cheddar.)
- ¾ cup grated Asiago
- ¾ cup grated Monterey Jack (Cheese grating is the perfect job for the sous-chef while you start the sauce.)
- 1 pound elbow macaroni, cooked and drained (My fav is Ronzoni.)
- 1 small box of grape tomatoes (Slice the tomatoes lengthwise—another great job for the sous-chef.)
- ½ cup fresh breadcrumbs

Garnish with:
- 1 Tablespoon fresh thyme leaves
- 1 Tablespoon fresh chives, chopped (Did I mention I LOVE chives? Except when they get caught in my teeth … remember to check a mirror after you eat this.)

Here's a prep tip if you're cooking minus the sexy sous-chef option: *mise en place*. That's the fancy French way of saying to have all your ingredients ready: measured and chopped and placed in small ramekins or a soufflé dish. You'll thank me later. I promise.

Preheat oven to 400 degrees Fahrenheit. Melt butter over medium heat in a large sauté pan. I use a 3.5-quart Cuisinart (start boiling the water for the macaroni at the same time following the directions on the box). Add onions and garlic. Cook until they are soft and onions are translucent, about 2-3 minutes. Add the flour and stir until the mixture turns light brown, usually takes less than 3 minutes for me. Gradually add milk as you stir.

This is the part where you dump in the spices from the small soufflé dish: paprika, nutmeg, salt and pepper. Reduce heat to low and cook. (You should have your macaroni in the water about now—al dente cooks in 7 minutes.)

Stir until the sauce thickens, about 5 minutes. Then add all three cheeses, and stir until they are melted.

Your macaroni needs to be done, drained and back in the pan by now. Pour the sauce from the sauté pan into the pot with the drained and cooked macaroni. Stir until the noodles are all coated with the cheesy mixture. It won't be super thick. My recipe is on the light side, so the sauce isn't thick and gooey.

Remove from the heat, pour the cheesy noodles into a pre-greased 9 x 13 baking dish.

Top with the sliced tomatoes (this is one of the best parts), and then sprinkle with breadcrumbs.

Bake until the cheese bubbles and turns golden brown, about 30 minutes.

Take the baking dish out of the oven and garnish with

chopped thyme and chives.

There you go! It's a crowd pleaser, I guarantee it. Believe it or not, paired with some bacon-wrapped mini-meatloaves and roasted asparagus, it's worthy of a dinner party. At least that's what our guests thought on New Year's Day.

Hey, thanks again for hanging out. If you want me to hook you up with the bacon-wrapped mini-meatloaf recipe, send me an e-mail to RainesRoost@gmail.com.

If you make the mac and cheese, tweet me or shoot me a line and let me know how it turned out for you.

Have a Mac-a-Tastic day, and take it easy until next time.

—Raine

Bonus: Mini-Meatloaf—Raine Style

This is crazy good with Mac-a-Tastic mac 'n' cheese and some roasted asparagus. Here it is cooked. This recipe normally makes 6 meatloaves, but we had a bunch of people on New Year's Day. This is really easy to make, and always a crowd pleaser. Veal mix is best, better than just beef—trust me on this one. You can ask the Butcher at your supermarket if you don't see it.

- 2 pounds Veal Mix chop meat (beef, veal, pork)
- 1 package of D'Artagnan Applewood smoked bacon (Oscar-Meyer will do too, but I like brands with no nitrates—much healthier. As healthy as bacon can be, if you know what I mean)
- ½ cup ketchup
- ½ cup breadcrumbs
- 1 onion
- 1 egg
- 1 clove garlic
- Salt to taste (about ½ teaspoon)
- Pepper to taste (about ¼ teaspoon)

Mix ingredients to form individual meatloaves (about 6), then wrap the bacon over the top to cover them. Bake for 1 hour at 350 degrees F. There you go. An easy-to-make dinner party.

Good luck!
—Raine

Chocolate-covered Strawberries
—à la Raine

This post originally appeared February 11, 2016 on the *USA TODAY* **Happy Ever After** Blog.

RAINE

Hey. Welcome back! Looks like I'll be here monthly for the rest of 2016. Sweet! My heartfelt thanks to all of you for your support and social media shares—especially those of you who made my recipes. You rock!

Since Valentine's Day is in a few days, I wanted a recipe that was holiday themed so anyone who makes it will look like a culinary rock star. It's easy and involves Jillian's favorite food group: chocolate. Plus some fruit. That's healthy. How can you go wrong? As long as no allergies are involved, you're golden.

Today's pick has a story behind it. It's no secret my mom taught me how to cook (through well-intentioned monetary bribes, also known as an allowance) starting when I turned ten. By the time she died when I was eighteen, I could feed myself more than Ramen noodles and toast.

I had my first real girlfriend at fifteen. Valentine's Day rolled around, and there I was, low on funds, agonizing over what to do. Mom shook her head, dragged me into the kitchen, and sat me on a stool. She told me the thought behind a gift was just as important as the gift itself, and she bet that we'd find all I needed in the kitchen and the greenhouse—yeah, we actually had one of those when I was growing up—to make something great. Of course I rolled my eyes and sulked. I'd been hoping for a loan and a trip to the mall. She clicked her tongue, and said, "What girl wouldn't appreciate flowers and chocolate?" She had a point.

Thirty minutes later, we had a dozen chocolate-covered strawberries. My mom was an artist and born in Sweden, so decoration was important to her. She insisted on dressing them up with white chocolate flakes. Me? I like them naked or covered in nuts. Anyway, my mom made a box and hand-painted it in her studio. We loaded up the chocolate berries after they hardened in the fridge, and paired them with a few tulips wrapped in a bow from the greenhouse. I was all set. Mom was right. My girlfriend at the time liked them ... *a lot*. It's also no secret that I lost my vir—forget it. That left unsaid, they've been in my arsenal as a strategic wooing tool ever since.

I'm going to surprise Jillian tonight with this batch. I'm thinking these and a glass of champagne in the soaking tub? Some candle action. Hmm ... What do you think?

So here we go ... No sexy sous-chef required, since that's who you're probably making these for. So, let's rock. As a nod to my mom, I got some of these pink and white chocolate curls from Kings as one of the decorations.

CHOCOLATE-COVERED STRAWBERRIES
—À LA RAINE

- 1 lb. strawberries, washed and patted dry (12-16. Try to get the ones with long stems. If you can't find them, choose the biggest ones available.)
- 8 oz. semisweet chocolate chips (I used Guittard 46% cacao semisweet. You can go with bittersweet, but I wouldn't do higher than 60% cacao. But that's just me.)
- ½ Tablespoon Crisco (Yup. You read that right. Sounds kind of disgusting, doesn't it? I know you might be thinking: "Is that really a food?" Just roll with me here. It makes the chocolate easier to work with, smoother, and doesn't affect the taste at all. You'll be thanking me later.)
- Parchment or wax paper (I used unbleached wax paper.)

Garnish with:
- Shredded coconut
- Crushed pistachios
- As a nod to my mom, white chocolate curls

Dump the chocolate chips into a microwavable dish. Glass is preferred. Microwave 1 minute 30 seconds.

Stir, and then add the ½ Tablespoon of Crisco. Microwave for another 20 seconds (if you have less than a 1,000-watt microwave oven, you might need more time—give it 20-second shots until the chocolate is melted).

Dip one strawberry at a time until coated with chocolate, and place on wax paper.

Repeat until all your strawberries are covered in chocolate.

Sprinkle on garnishes of your choice, and then refrigerate for 1 hour.

Good for a few days … if they last that long.

Voilà, here they are:

NAKED   For HER   For HIM

Good luck! Guaranteed to impress, and hopefully … you know … get your partner (or sous-chef) *ahem* in the mood.

Have a happy Valentine's Day, and take it easy until next time.

—Raine

Chicken Tortilla Soup & Easy Guac

This post originally appeared March 9, 2016 on the *USA TODAY* **Happy Ever After** Blog.

RAINE

So what did you guys think of the Oscars? Jillian and I are catching up on all the movies we missed before the Academy Awards. The weather in the Northeast has been like a roller coaster between warm days and "freeze your *cojones* off" cold. Nights like that, I like easy-to-make soup. Today's recipe is one of my new "go-to" soups ... well, not really new if you look at the date on the magazine I found it in. I think you all know by now that Jillian hates cooking almost as much as she hates spiders, but that never stopped her from saving recipes from magazines on the off chance she'd wake up one day and decide to use her expensive crockery. After I moved in with her, I found her secret stash of neatly clipped recipes. I had her pull a few she wanted to try ... this was one of them. It's from a magazine that went out of circulation years ago, and this is my take.

I made it for our viewing of *The Big Short* the other night. Christian Bale, Brad Pitt and Steve Carell were brilliant. You should see it if you haven't already. I'm still amazed people got away with buying homes using their dog's identity. Go figure. Only in America. The mortgage crisis was the beginning of the end of my dad's career … Uh, yeah, on to happier thoughts.

Even though I was fresh out of tortilla chips, I made this recipe anyway. They're optional, and you don't really need them for the soup. Lucky we had some crostini crackers in the house (they rock, by the way), because they're great with guacamole. Mine is bare bones with just the key ingredients—since it's all I had in the fridge the first time I made it. You won't miss all the bells and whistles, trust me. Try it once this way, and you'll never go back. I haven't. So here goes …

CHICKEN TORTILLA SOUP

- 1 large onion, diced (Remember I told you in January that my onion dicer died? Now that I've been turned on to the fresh, diced organic onions in the produce aisle at Kings, I'm addicted. They're like a drug, I can't give them up. Saves me time and burning, bleary eyes. (¼ container = approx. 1 onion))
- 1 Tablespoon ground cumin
- 1 Tablespoon cooking oil
- 28 oz. box of reduced-sodium chicken broth (This is a good way to cut the salt, since there are other ingredients in this recipe that contribute to the sodium content.)
- 28 oz. can fire-roasted diced tomatoes (The best is Muir Glen. They come with and without chilies. Since Jillian doesn't like it too spicy, I use 1 14 oz. can with chilies, and one without then skip the 8 oz. can of green chilies that's listed below.)
- 4 cups chicken, cooked and chopped (My favorite short-cut—use rotisserie chicken from the supermarket deli.)
- 10 oz. package of sweet whole kernel corn (frozen or organic canned)
- 8 oz. can (or two 4 oz. cans) diced green chile peppers

Garnish with any or all of these:
- Tortilla chips or strips
- Shredded cheddar
- Fresh cilantro
- Diced avocado
- Grape tomatoes
- Lime

Use a 5- to 6-quart Dutch oven or deep pot that you'd use for making pasta.

Cook onion and cumin in hot oil over medium heat for 5 minutes, or until onions are translucent. Stir and keep stirring. Then add the broth, undrained tomatoes, chicken, corn and undrained chilies.

Bring to a boil, and then reduce the heat and simmer (covered) for 15 minutes. It's fine to simmer longer to mix the flavors.

Garnish with anything from the list above. I'm into cheddar and avocado.

It's good as leftovers for a couple of days.

EASIEST GUAC ON THE PLANET & CHIPS
(WELL, ACTUALLY CROSTINI)

- 1 large avocado
- 1 lime (used it for the soup)
- Pink Himalayan salt to taste
- Fresh ground black pepper to taste
- In place of chips, use crostini crackers (or any other cracker of choice)

Cut avocado in half, discard pit. Score the avocado crossways and then lengthwise while still in the skin to make cubes. Squeeze the skin, and cubes should pop out. If not, use a knife to loosen avocado from the skin, then squeeze contents into a bowl.

Cut a wedge of lime and squeeze over avocado cubes.

My salt has a grinder, so grind some salt over the top—be careful you don't overdo it. The same goes for pepper.

Mash together with a fork and get an even consistency. I leave mine on the chunky side.

There you go. This is great for a cold night when you're tapped for time. And it's a gift that keeps on giving. There's usually enough soup for the next day or two. Jillian and I will do a "twofer," and I'll freeze the rest for another time.

Try it. It's quick, easy and, for the diet-conscious, low-cal.

Take care until next time, and happy cooking.
—Raine

Cheddar & Bacon Egg Strata

This post originally appeared April 14, 2016 on the *USA TODAY* **Happy Ever After** Blog.

RAINE

Hey. What's up? Thanks for stopping by to check out this month's recipe, or in my words, "my idea on how to keep your significant other from a steady diet of cold cereal and chocolate." In between gigs, you can find me on Twitter (@ Raines_Roost). Just tweet me if you have any questions, want to say hi, or to just check out my latest comments on ManU. Any soccer fans out there?

This month, I'm going to share a brunch recipe that I adapted, or should I say "Americanized," from my Mom's Swedish version of an egg strata … She used to make it Easter morning. Her recipe had Gravlax (cured salmon) and Greve (Swedish Baby Swiss), which I still make … sometimes … for myself. Jillian's not a fan of smoked salmon. Too salty. This is our compromise: cheddar and bacon. Honestly? You can toss in anything you'd normally put in an omelet, and it would taste fine. Depending on what it is, you might have to pre-cook it. Not this, just toss it in "as is." If you like fish, give it a whirl with my mom's ingredients.

But here's the rub, and why I save it for a morning I need to cook for guests, or a holiday (like Christmas or Easter), or both (like this year): You need to prep it no less than eight hours (up to 24) in advance. Trust me, it's worth the wait. Prep time is short. I make it before bed and put it in the fridge. You can throw together the ingredients in about 10 minutes as long as you buy pre-cooked bacon and don't make croutons from scratch.

CHEDDAR & BACON EGG STRATA

- 4 oz. French bread, ¾-inch cubes (4 cups) (I get the fresh—Ha! Sounds better than stale—bread cubes they sell at the supermarket from their day-old bread, but you can just pick up your favorite unseasoned brand.)
- 1½ cups shredded cheddar cheese (The pre-shredded stuff rocks.)
- 4 slices bacon, crisp-cooked and crumbled (Pre-cooked, no nitrates, 15 seconds in the microwave does the trick for me.)
- 2 cups milk
- 4 eggs, beaten
- 1 teaspoon cut fresh chives ('Tis the season—or it was—I have a pot outside that just froze over two nights ago with the Polar Vortex—freaking weather!)
- ½ teaspoon mustard (I like Dijon.)
- ¼ teaspoon ground black pepper
- ¼ teaspoon Herbes de Provence (Optional—but I've been addicted to them since Jillian and I went to France.)
- Pinch of onion powder (about 1/8 of a teaspoon)

Toss together the bread cubes, cheddar cheese and cooked, crumbled bacon in a large bowl.

You can either use six individual 10-ounce ramekins or a two-quart soufflé dish (this is my go-to). Put bread-cheese-bacon mixture into dish or dishes of choice.

In a medium bowl, whisk together the milk, eggs, chives,

mustard, black pepper, Herbes de Provence and onion powder.

Pour it over the bread mixture already in the dish(es).

Cover and refrigerate for 8-24 hours.

When you're ready, bake, uncovered, for 25-30 minutes at 350 degrees Fahrenheit if you use the small dishes. If you use the big kahuna (two-quart) keep it in the oven for 40-45 minutes. You can check it by inserting a knife, and if it comes out clean, you're golden.

Let it cool for five minutes. Serve it up with cut fruit. Makes enough for six.

There you go. Jillian's sister Kitty and her husband, Bob, dropped in before church on Easter for brunch. She asked for the recipe ... with the fish. Unlike Jillian, turns out she loves smoked fish. Wasn't a morsel left when we finished. Maybe I should revise the serving estimate: enough for four hungry and enthusiastic adults. Try it. Impress your friends and family.

Before I go, I hope Joyce doesn't mind, but I'm going to throw in a shameless plug for a friend. Check it out. If you're reading this recipe when it first posts, on April 14, 2016, and you're at some big romance convention called RT Booklovers in Vegas, find our girl, L.G. O'Connor. She's a friend of the family. Jillian says she's raffling off a pair of those fancy heels with red soles. Me? Heels are heels. As long as Jillian's wearing them, that's all that matters. The higher the better and preferably alone. Ha! You know what I'm talkin' about. Hold up …

Jillian just gave me a little elbow-to-rib action, told me I was "such a guy" and asked me to take out the last two lines. I gave her a look and quoted the First Amendment. She chuckled and walked away. So find L.G. … I hear she's selling some advance copies of *Caught Up in Raine* at the Book Fair before it launches Monday. *That* you won't want to miss, I guarantee it.

Cook on,
—Raine

Glazed Salmon, meal-in-a-pan

This post originally appeared May 12, 2016 on the *USA TODAY* **Happy Ever After** Blog.

RAINE

Hey there. Welcome back to Raine's Roost. This month, I have a guest sous-chef … Nope, it's not Jillian. She's in her office on a book deadline but promised to join us for dinner when we're done. Any other guesses? No? It's Jillian's niece, Jenny. She asked (um, actually she begged) me to hook her up with an easy recipe that she can make for her first dinner party. Tonight's the test run.

Now, if I can just get her to understand the difference between a teaspoon and a tablespoon, we'll be golden. That and how to cook without the assistance of a fire extinguisher … For the record, she just gave me a dirty look, which would be warranted if I wasn't telling the God's honest truth. But, hey, I wasn't the one who almost blew her boyfriend's blood pressure off the charts by dropping a full tablespoon of salt into the last meal she cooked—after she set off the smoke alarm. Twice. Just sayin'.

So, in an effort to save her from having to call Domino's

pizza (or the fire department) to rescue her night, I'm taking her under my culinary wing.

To make this easy, I'm going to teach her a "one-pan" dish, kind of. This is served over greens, which are wilted in a separate pan while the salmon is cooking—but the same glaze is used on the whole meal. So, it's not really all in one pan, but I think you get it.

All that said, I usually make this meal for four (I'm a two-portion kind of guy, and cooking for three screws with my head), but since Jenny asked how to scale it back to two in the future for just her and her boyfriend, I'll explain how to slide this recipe from two to six servings. That should cover everyone. Cool? Cool.

Glazed salmon: Meal-in-a-pan
(serves two to four)

- ¼ cup Dijon mustard (for six servings, increase to 3/8 cup)
- ¼ cup vegetable oil (for six servings, increase to 3/8 cup)
- ¼ cup chopped fresh dill (for six servings, increase to 3/8 cup)
- 3 Tablespoons packed light brown sugar (for six servings, increase to ¼ cup)
- ½ pound baby new potatoes, cut into quarters (I use little net bags of multicolored potatoes—which make it look

nice. If you are serving four, increase to ¾ pound, for six, make it a full 1 pound.)

- Two 8-ounce salmon fillets (If you make it for four people, just double the fish—nothing else. For six, follow the instructions above for six servings.)
- ¾ bag of spinach (You can also use collard greens. For six servings, use the full bag.)

Preheat oven to 350 degrees F. Mix Dijon mustard, oil, dill and brown sugar together in a small bowl (can be made two hours ahead). Cover and let stand at room temperature.

Place potatoes in a small bowl and toss with 1 Tablespoon of sauce (for four servings, use 1.5 Tablespoons; for six servings, use 2 Tablespoons) until potatoes are coated.

Arrange potatoes flat on a baking pan and bake for 30 minutes.
Remove pan from oven; push potatoes to the sides of the pan.

Add the salmon fillets to the center of the baking pan and spread 1 teaspoon of sauce over each fillet. Bake until salmon is cooked through, about 23 minutes.

While the salmon is cooking, place spinach in a large skillet and toss with 2 Tablespoons of the sauce. Stir over medium-high heat until wilted—about four minutes.

Divide salmon, greens and potatoes between the plates. Serve, and pass the remaining sauce. If you are serving six, you might not have much left over, but you don't really need it. Jenny and I made the dish for six.

That's it. Notice anything odd about the photo? Yup. No greens. Turns out, Jenny picked up a bag of baby romaine instead of spinach. The perils of yakking on your cell while food shopping. Anyway, a nice alternative to the cooked spinach is a salad with goat cheese crumbles, dried cranberries and candied pecans (it's what I could scrape together between the fridge and the pantry.) Add a little balsamic dressing, and you're good to go. Turns out her boyfriend doesn't really love cooked greens, so I guess she'll do fine.

Despite the spinach snafu, she didn't need a fire extinguisher. I guess you could say that's progress.

Cook on, and see you next month.
—Raine

Shrimp & Orzo

This post first appeared June 9, 2016 on the *USA **Today*** **Happy Ever After** Blog.

RAINE

Hey, what's up? Welcome back. This month Raine's Roost is coming to you from my alternate perch at the Jersey Shore, Jillian's house in Spring Lake. This is where we'll be for the summer, so expect a lot of seafood and farmer's market dishes.

To get into the groove, I picked one of Jillian's favorites. One, because the shrimp looked good at the seafood market, and two, I was dying to try my new lemon squeezer (below). I know. I'm a total geek when it comes to kitchen utensils. There's actually a third reason, too—you get to drink the leftover white wine. So buy a good one.

Anyway, a good friend of Jillian's made this recipe for her years ago. On one of the rare occasions Jillian attempted to cook—trust me, a less than good idea—she picked this one. It's one of the times I was head's down with school and work, and a step away from losing my *shi*—mind. PBJs were pretty popular that week. She tried to surprise me, which I thoroughly appreciated. *Thoroughly. Appreciated.* No questions. I'll leave it to your imagination.

That said, it's not really her fault that my lips pulled into a wicked pucker when I tasted it. The recipe she'd transcribed didn't include some of the measurements—like how much lemon juice to use—so I've adapted it by taste, intuition and common sense.

One of the reasons I love this recipe? It's simple, elegant, and good enough for company. Plus, it makes a decent leftover. The flavors meld and absorb into the orzo after a few hours, making the dish just as good the second day. I tend to rely on the grill in summer, but the weather has been a mix of warm during the day and chilly at night here since Memorial Day, so making something warm and eating it cold for lunch the next day is all good in my book. Then there's the wine. I didn't drink wine much until I met Jillian. She's made me a convert.

So, you ready? Then buckle up …

SHRIMP & ORZO (SERVES 4)

- 8 ounces Orzo pasta (looks kind of like rice)
- 1 Tablespoon plus 1 teaspoon olive oil
- 2 cloves garlic
- 20 large shrimp, uncooked, deveined and unfrozen
- ½ teaspoon salt
- ¼ teaspoon pepper
- ¼ cup parsley (Cook 2 Tablespoons with shrimp then save the rest for the end.)
- 1 cup dry white wine (I picked up a 2015 Fog Mountain Sauvignon Blanc—good enough so we could finish it with dinner.)
- 2 Tablespoons fresh lemon juice
- 4 Tablespoons unsalted butter
- 1 Tablespoon capers, rinsed
- Lemon zest

Bring 4-5 quarts of water to a boil. Add a pinch of salt.

Boil orzo pasta until *al dente*—follow instructions on the box, about nine minutes.

Drain and transfer to a large bowl. Toss with 1 teaspoon of olive oil.

Heat remaining oil (1 Tablespoon) in a large skillet. Toss in the garlic and cook over medium heat for one minute.

Add unfrozen shrimp, sprinkle salt, pepper and 2 Tablespoons of parsley over the shrimp, and cook for three to four minutes or until the shrimp is opaque (turning from gray to pinkish.)

When the shrimp are done, pluck them out of the pan one at a time and keep them warm in another bowl.

Don't get rid of what's in the pan. You need it. Then add lemon juice and wine. Turn up the heat and bring to a boil. Lower the heat after it reaches a boil, and then reduce the liquid contents in the pan by about half (takes about two to four minutes).

Once the liquid in the pan is reduced, turn off the heat, and add the remaining parsley. Stir in butter, lemon zest and washed capers.

Give the juice a taste, and adjust seasonings if necessary. If it's good, pour it over shrimp. Then serve the shrimp on a bed of orzo with the pan juice. There you go...

It's warm enough tonight to take a walk on the beach after dinner. I highly recommend it. Oh, and grab that bottle of Fog Mountain and a blanket on the way out. Add stars, night sky and imagination ...

Thanks for hanging out. Take care until next month.
—Raine

Crab Deviled Eggs—à la Raine

This post first appeared July 14, 2016 on the USA TODAY Happy Ever After Blog.

RAINE

Hey, happy summer from the Jersey Shore! I'm coming at you again from Raine's Roost South, the mecca of all things seafood and farmer's market fresh. Jillian and I are enjoying month number two at our house in Spring Lake. My apologies in advance to anyone with fish allergies or who can't stare a sockeye, well, in the *eye*. OK, bad analogy. Translation: hates fish or avoids it for religious reasons. If that's the case, for this recipe just leave out the crab and cut the mayo.

July is a big entertainment month for us, mostly driven by the magic ingredient of owning a house on the beach. That and we like to hang out with friends and family when Jillian's not on a deadline. She's taking a research break before she starts her new novel. Something set down here in Spring Lake about an antiques dealer and an FBI agent. As part of her research, she's been creeping around dusty old antiques shops. It's kind of spurred this new obsession of hers to find vintage kitchenware and rooster-related items for our two kitchens. Anyway, I'm featuring one of her latest treasures in today's post. It's cute, right? On the same trip to Red Bank that Jillian found the egg plate, she came home with a 19th-century ceramic rooster. I unwrapped it and noticed the sticker on the bottom, "19c Staffordshire Cock." It gave me a good laugh and drew an arched brow from her. *Was that a hint?* There were just too many ways I could take a metaphor ... Instead, I gave Jillian a "thank-you" kiss she'll likely never forget and let her know she was welcome to check out my growing rooster collection whenever she had the urge. *Ahem.* Moving on to the recipe ...

Besides getting to showcase my vintage rooster egg dish, this recipe was a special request from our latest guests, Jillian's literary agent, Brigitte, and her husband, Richard. They came to visit this past weekend. She's my girl's girl, and has a special place in my heart for all she's done for me and Jillian. Richard's cool. He's a wine importer in New York. So, as you can probably imagine, we had good wine with every meal but breakfast.

After a little too much sun and vino for all involved, Brigitte egged me on (pun intended) to make crab deviled eggs ... from scratch. My first response? *"Are you insane?"* I caved to all of her pleading when we finally made it to the fishmonger. For the record, I only agreed because she volunteered to help me pick the meat out of the shells.

One word: nightmare. If you decide to go with the fresh crab, one piece of advice: Don't be hungry when you make these. But it's worth it as far as taste. Ready to go? Great.

CRAB DEVILED EGGS À LA RAINE

- 12 hard-cooked large eggs
- Meat from 9 cooked Blue crabs OR 1 can (6 ounces) crabmeat, drained, flaked and cartilage removed
- 1/2 cup mayonnaise
- 2 green onions, finely chopped (aka scallions)
- 2 teaspoons Dijon mustard
- 1/2 teaspoon salt
- 1/8 teaspoon pepper
- 3 dashes of Frank's Red Hot (This is my favorite hot pepper sauce, but it doesn't really come out in a dash, so sprinkle it to taste, 10 small dots works for me. You might want to try 5-7 to start.)

- 3 dashes of Worcestershire sauce
- Chives, finely chopped
- Paprika

The secret to making these is prepping the eggs so the shells come off without sticking. It's easy. Boil 3-4 quarts of water. Once it's at a rolling boil, place eggs in for 12 minutes.

Scoop eggs out of the boiling water when the timer goes off, and place into another bowl. Cover the eggs with cold water. Let them sit submerged for 20 minutes.

Tap the smaller (pointy) end of the egg on the counter, and start to peel from there.

Cut eggs lengthwise, and carefully pop out the yolks into a bowl. Add to the yolks: crab, scallions, mayo, mustard, Frank's, Worcestershire, salt, and pepper. Mix until consistent.

Scoop crab mixture into the hollowed out egg whites. I use two spoons to control it. This stuff is too thick to pipe out of a pastry nozzle. Garnish with chives & paprika. Voila!

Looking for a wine pairing? We had them with a great Pinot Gris straight from Richard's wine cellar.

Thanks for hanging out!
Peace,
—Raine

Yellow Watermelon & Tomato Salad with Lime & Honey Vinaigrette

This post first appeared August 11, 2016 on the **USA *Today* Happy Ever After** Blog.

RAINE

How's it going? I've got something special for you this month: Raine's Roost is on the road. Yup, you heard that right. Coming to you from one of the most amazing places on the planet—the Russian River Valley in Sonoma County, California. This month is farm-to-table all the way.

Jillian had a business trip out this way, so we decided to visit one of Jillian's good friends and her husband and make a little vacation out of it. With this month's recipe, you'll get an added benefit—some extra pictures of my foodie tour through town and where we stayed. Thanks in advance for the indulgence and letting me share.

If you read last month's post, then you'll remember that Brigitte and Richard visited us down in Spring Lake, and that Richard is a wine merchant. Having been a bartender on and off for the three years before I'd met Jillian, my choices used to gravitate between mixed drinks and beer. Since then, I've grown an appreciation for wine, especially after a few lessons from Richard in wine tasting. Anyway, when Jillian mentioned a writer's conference in San Francisco and suggested a few days to visit friends in Healdsburg, I jumped at the chance. Turns out her friend Anneke's husband, Jack, likes to cook as much as I do ... and the man has his own outdoor pizza oven. Like, how sick good is that?

First of all, if you've never been to the town of Healdsburg, run, don't walk. Our hosts were throwing a dinner party Saturday night, so of course I offered to prepare one of my favorites: watermelon and yellow tomato salad with mint and lime/honey vinaigrette. It's easy and a guaranteed crowd pleaser. So, our first stop that morning was the farmer's market. Holy crap! If we had one this great in New Jersey, I'd freaking live there. I got teary-eyed just looking at all the produce.

After loading up like a pack mule with our haul, I made a stop by the car to unload, and we all headed to brunch at

Shed. After my rhapsody with the farmer's market, I didn't think it could get much better. Wrong. *Effing hell.* I felt like I died and went to foodie heaven. Just walking in the door practically got me as excited as seeing Jillian naked. Sorry if that's TMI, but for someone like me who loves food, you need to understand what I'm talkin' about. Just saying. It's a combo café, restaurant, food store. Some pics for you:

My lunch—Spanish white anchovies with Meyer lemon Aioli and radish. Unbelievable.

We stopped at the Plaza Gourmet kitchen store before leaving town to go back up the mountain. I bought so much stuff I had to get it shipped home. So, again, if you read last month's post, you know that Jillian's on a quest to build a collection of my kitchen's mascot. But I had to laugh with appreciation when I saw this cookbook. One picture from Jillian, and one from me:

Guess whose is whose? LOL.

Another thing before I dive in. This recipe morphed on the spot the moment I cut open the watermelon and saw that it was ... yellow. And it had seeds. Yeah. Not what I expected. This is meant to be a red watermelon recipe, but what the hell. It turned out to be sweet and delicious, and didn't stop anyone from devouring it. And, if I'm allowed to say so, it was effing fantastic. OK, enough digression, time to get down to business ...

Yellow watermelon & tomato salad with lime & honey vinaigrette

- 1 small-medium watermelon
- 6-8 small-medium heirloom tomatoes (if you have red watermelon, they should be yellow tomatoes, but I picked up a variety which saved my ass from an entire palette of yellow on the plate)
- Ricotta Salata cheese (this is a very firm white cheese)
- Fresh mint

Vinaigrette:
- 1 lime
- 1 Tablespoon of honey
- 1 pinch of cayenne pepper
- 1/4 cup olive oil

Cut watermelon in thin slices and arrange on a plate. Then cut tomatoes (wash them first) into small wedges, and place them on top of the watermelon.

Shave the ricotta salata cheese (with a cheese slicer) into thick curls over the top of the watermelon & tomatoes.

In a small bowl, add the juice of a whole lime, honey, olive oil, and cayenne pepper. Whisk together until smooth and consistent.

Drizzle over watermelon and tomatoes, and garnish with mint leaves (we got these fresh from Jack's garden). Makes enough for eight.

The plate was clean by the time dessert was served. Enjoy!

We had dinner on the patio overlooking the pool and the mountains.

Jack made a ton of pizzas in the oven, served with the watermelon salad, a carrot salad and a simple green salad—all compliments of his garden or our trip to the farmer's market.

The nights get cool here, so we eventually went inside for tea and coffee.

After everyone left, we ended the night in the hot tub. Now that's what I call "living your best life." Jillian agrees.

Stay cool, and enjoy the rest of your summer. Peace.
—Raine

Herb & Heirloom Tomato Tart

This post first appeared September 8, 2016 on the *USA Today* **Happy Ever After** Blog.

RAINE

Hey, welcome back for my last summer recipe of the season. OK, I know you can make a tart any time of the year, but to get the best heirloom tomatoes, you need to make it now.

If you missed last month's post, live from the Russian River Valley in Sonoma County, California, you need to check it out. Then you'll understand why I've been obsessed with heirloom tomatoes. I've always been a big fan, but even more now.

Just a reminder that the purpose of my posts is to provide easy, "go-to" recipes that anyone can make to come out looking like a rock star in the kitchen. That, and keeping your significant other from living on yogurt and ice cream. Trust me, this one will help.

Here in northern New Jersey, we're already feeling a few notes of fall. Here's hoping we have another mild September. Jillian and I made the most out of our summer this year outside of work. That meant a ton of entertaining, beach time and just enough travel to keep us satisfied. I'll admit, I'm rocking a pretty decent tan right now, and I'd rather be manning the grill than the stove as we enjoy the last days of summer.

I'm not sure about you, but the heat steals my appetite. This summer we changed our meal pattern on the weekends from three meals a day to two: late morning and late afternoon with a snack at night if we're hungry. With that in mind, having something substantial with protein to start the day makes it work. One solution? Tarts, as long as you're not lactose intolerant. They don't take long, especially if you get uncooked pie shells and pre-grated fresh cheese. Prep time is 10-15 minutes. You can also make them the night before. Just pop it in the oven and watch a movie while it cooks.

Here we go, time to get busy ...

HERB AND HEIRLOOM TOMATO TART

- 9-inch unbaked tart shell, chilled (I use Oronoque Orchards)
- 2 Tablespoons unsalted butter
- 1 heaping teaspoon each of fresh herbs: chives, thyme, parsley and basil
- 6-8 heirloom cherry tomatoes, cut in quarters
- 2 eggs and 2 egg yolks
- 2 cups heavy cream or 1 cup heavy cream and 1 cup whole milk (I like to cut the fat, so I use the milk combo)
- 1 cup Gruyere cheese, grated
- Salt, pepper, nutmeg—to taste

Preheat oven to 375 degrees F. Heat butter in a skillet to melt, and then add herbs and tomato quarters. Stir briefly, about a minute.

In a large bowl, whip eggs, yolks, cream or cream/milk combo. Season egg mixture with salt and pepper, then add a hint of ground nutmeg.

Stir the herb/tomato mixture into the egg mixture, and pour into tart shell.

Cook on middle rack on a tray about 45-55 minutes (milk mixture takes on the longer side). Let cool for 20 minutes before serving. Enough for 6.

I'm in love with these micro greens. Any salad served with a vinaigrette will do, but these cutie pies are a favorite with a white balsamic dressing I get from the local gourmet shop downtown.

So, as sad as I am to say goodbye to summer, there are a couple of things I like about fall. English Premiership soccer. Go ManU. I'm looking forward to seeing what Jose Moreno has in store as their new coach. Besides that, cider doughnuts from Wightman's Farm in Morristown.

See you next month. Peace.
—Raine

Rosemary-Lemon Chicken Thighs

This post first appeared October 13, 2016 on the **USA *Today* Happy Ever After** Blog.

RAINE

Hey, thanks for stopping by to check out my first fall recipe. This is one of my favorites. What can I say? I'm a thigh man, especially when it comes to chicken. But really, the prep on this recipe is so quick and hard to screw up ... unless you're the love of my life, Jillian. Then all bets are off. As much as I adore her (and her thighs), she's the first to admit that she could burn water.

Fall. Wow. It was just summer ... like last week. Now there's dead leaves scattered on the grass, and down the road in Harding the trees are turning. With the remnants of Hurricane Matthew blowing a chilly breeze through New Jersey this weekend, I had a craving for some comfort food. To prepare for colder weather, we bought a conversion kit to turn one of our fireplaces into gas. I may be King of the Kitchen, but pyrotechnics in the fireplace is a different story. Jillian still hasn't forgiven me for setting off the smoke alarm last season when I tried to coax a fire along with a pinch of lighter fluid. Stupid. Yeah, I know. I had to paint over the soot it left on the mantel. She gave away the rest of the wood so I wouldn't be tempted to do it again. Too bad the plumber the fireplace store promised to send three weeks ago has been MIA. At this rate, I'm hoping he gets here before Halloween. Then again, it's supposed to be 75 degrees again this week. Go figure.

But I digress. If you want something awesome to serve with your chicken thighs, let me suggest my Mac-a-Tastic mac and cheese recipe from January. Just add a green salad and you're good to go.

As a nod to fall, I went a little wild on the herbs (Ha! Not really.). Usually, this recipe calls for just rosemary, but then I spotted the poultry mix with sage, rosemary and thyme. Only a sprig of parsley away from a Simon & Garfunkel tune. Going wild would've been adding the parsley. Time to get busy …

ROSEMARY-LEMON CHICKEN THIGHS

- 6 chicken thighs
- 1 large lemon
- Fresh rosemary OR mix sage, rosemary and thyme (That's what I used this time.)
- ¼ cup olive oil
- ½ Tablespoon salt (Kosher is the best.)
- ½ Tablespoon garlic, chopped

Preheat oven to 425 degrees F. Line a 9-by-13 rectangular baking pan with foil (I use metal pans). I recommend using one with a removable elevated insert. Don't worry if you don't have one, but use the foil either way to catch all the drippings. Makes clean-up a snap.

Cut lemon into 6 round slices and place evenly around the bottom of the foil-lined pan.

Place a chicken thigh (leave skin on) on top of each lemon slice.

Mix olive oil, salt, garlic. Add leaves from 3-4 sprigs of rosemary and 3-4 sprigs of thyme into the olive oil mixture.

Brush mixture over the chick thighs to coat, and then top each thigh with a sprig each of rosemary and thyme. On top of that, add two torn sage leaves.

Cook on middle rack for 1 hour.

Enjoy the rest of your October. One of my favorite holidays as a kid was Halloween … it still is. My favorite candy? 3 Musketeers. Frozen. What's yours?

Later. Peace.
—Raine

Chestnut, Apple and Sausage Stuffing, Raine-style

This post first appeared November 10, 2016 on the **USA Today Happy Ever After** Blog.

RAINE

Hey, what's up? Glad you could swing by to see what's cooking in the Roost. With Thanksgiving just around the corner, I decided to share the centerpiece of my Thanksgiving dinner—my absolute favorite stuffing of all time. I cook it outside the bird in a pan. I don't stuff my turkeys, so I can't offer any advice there.

Last month, fall was just gearing up here, but now it's in full swing. We have maples, and there's nothing more spectacular than those deep-red leaves. If I look out our kitchen window, we've got a palette of red, yellow and green that's out of this world. For those who read last month's post, the gas fireplace is fully installed. The whoosh of a fire is only half a knob turn away, and we've been rocking some good flames every night this week. *Best. Thing. Ever.* Also from last month, I'm not so happy to report that we still have 18 pounds of Halloween candy left. Lesson learned by Jillian:

Don't send Raine to buy the candy.

Since this is November and, for all intents and purposes, a Thanksgiving post, I figured I'd share the story of my first Thanksgiving with Jillian. When Jillian's kitchen was still her kitchen and not my exclusive domain. Before the Roost was the Roost. The very first time Jillian volunteered to be my sexy sous-chef.

Enjoy, and meet you on the other side …

(Disclaimer: The passage below mentions the Food Network—L.G. took some literary license for the book. My recipes don't come from there. Other than that, this scene is an accurate depiction.)

EXCERPT from *Caught Up in Raine.*
Copyright © 2016 by L.G. O'Connor. Used with permission.

I'm running around the kitchen like a lunatic with the Macy's Thanksgiving Day parade on TV in the background. Underdog and Hello Kitty float by on the screen, keeping me company while I scramble around, hyperventilating. Why did I think it was good idea to invite Jillian's family to her house for Thanksgiving? The bigger question is: Why on earth did I think I could make the whole meal from scratch?

The turkey is safely in the oven, but the counter is covered in the ingredients I need for stuffing, cranberry sauce, apple and pear pies, and a sweet potato puree that I thought looked good. My laptop is open to the Food Network, and all the bookmarked recipes I found earlier this week are lined up in memory.

My fingers are woven into my hair, and I'm wearing a look of panic when Jillian comes into the kitchen. I'm about thirty seconds away from screaming at the top of my lungs.

Her face screws up in a frown. "Raine, are you okay? You look like you're about to snap."

"I need help," I say, feeling like a drowning man clutching for a life preserver.

She comes over to me and places her hands on my shoulders. Her golden eyes lock me in her gaze. "Relax. I'll help you. Take two deep breaths."

I blow my breath in and out twice. "Done."

"Feel better?"

"No."

"Sit." She chuckles and points to the stool.

I sit. She walks over to get a pen and paper and then settles down beside me.

"Calmly, tell me the temperature of the turkey and how long it takes," she says.

"350 degrees for six hours," I say, wringing my hands and bouncing my knee nervously up and down. "I put it in at eight a.m."

She jots it down. "Okay, tell me what else you're going to make, include the time it takes and the temperature." I recite my list of side dishes and desserts including the specifics she asked for with the help of the recipes on my laptop.

Done, she hands me the list. Thank God for double ovens. There's a grid of both ovens with start times, end times, and prep times all calculated.

"This is amazing," I say as I watch her roll up her sleeves and wash her hands.

"I'm going to be your sous-chef," she says. "Let's start on the sweet potatoes first, since they take the most prep."

My eyebrows fly up. "Have you been holding out on me?"

She chuckles. "My planning is great; it's my food that tastes like crap. Together, I think we'll be a kick-ass team and make a decent meal. Ready?"

I pull her into my arms and growl into her neck. "I love you."

"Hey, that tickles." She giggles, and clenches her shoulders up to protect her neck. "Love you, too. Now, let's get crackin'."

So there you have it folks, my maiden Thanksgiving voyage. By the way, the meal turned out great. It's what happens afterward that will make your hair fly. Catch our whole story, in the *Caught Up in Raine Collection*, exclusively on Amazon. Time to get cooking …

CHESTNUT, APPLE AND SAUSAGE STUFFING, RAINE-STYLE

- 12 oz. bag, Martin's soft cubed potato bread OR any other unseasoned croutons
- ½ lb. bulk chicken or pork sausage
- 4 Tbs. (1/2 stick) unsalted butter
- 1 yellow onion, chopped (King's diced onions in the produce aisle save me the tears.)
- 3 large stalks of celery, chopped
- 2 Granny Smith apples, cored and chopped (I use the thing that sections and cores at the same time, then cut each section into 3-4 pieces.)
- 3 Tbs. fresh thyme, chopped
- ¾ cup low-sodium chicken broth
- 15 oz. jar of prepared chestnuts, roughly chopped
- ½ cup fresh parsley, chopped
- Salt & freshly ground pepper to taste
- 2 eggs, beaten and blended in a bowl

Remember I mentioned *mis en place* (having your ingredients chopped, diced, and pre-measured into small dishes ready to go) in a prior post? I highly recommend it for this recipe.

Preheat oven to 325 degrees F, and grease a 9 x 13 glass or ceramic pan.

Dump the bread cubes into a large mixing bowl (I use the largest one I own—trust me, you'll need the space).
Cook sausage in a large frying pan over medium heat, stir occasionally, until browned (10-12 minutes). Add sausage to bread cubes in the bowl.

Melt butter in a large sauté pan, add chopped onions and chopped celery, stir occasionally, until tender (6-8 minutes). Then add apples, thyme and chicken broth to pan. Cook 2-3 minutes, scraping up any browned bits.

Add pan mixture to bowl along with chestnuts, parsley, salt and pepper to taste, stir to blend. Add eggs and mix again (if it looks a little dry, I add ¼ cup more broth to it).

Spoon mixture from bowl to pan, cover with foil. Cook for 30 minutes, remove foil and cook for another 30 minutes.

Have a Happy Thanksgiving!
Gobble-gobble,
—Raine

Not-so-green Holly Cookies

This post first appeared December 8, 2016 on the *USA Today* **Happy Ever After** Blog.

RAINE

Hey, how's it going? Thanks for your support and dropping by to see what's been cooking in the Roost over the last year. A huge "thank you" to Joyce Lamb, who's allowed me to do a baker's dozen worth of recipe takeovers since last December in her column. Sharing recipes and some snippets about my life with Jillian pre- and post-*Caught Up in Raine* has been a blast! Thanks for all your support; I truly appreciate it. For real.

I'll be wrapping up my gig here with a McNally family (Jillian's maiden name) favorite for Christmas. I put today's recipe choice to a vote with Jillian, my niece Jenny (Ha! Still feel funny calling her that since she's only two years younger than me), and her sister Kitty, and they chose this one. If you've been following my column, you know I steer toward the healthier side of food. But with something like this, there weren't a lot of healthy places I could go with butter and sugar. Still, that didn't stop me from dropping my stamp on the recipe.

When Jillian and Kitty were growing up, their favorite Christmas cookies were these neon green holly cookies made with marshmallows, Cornflakes and red-hot candies. Yikes! I know, I know, they taste good. I'm just sayin' that food that green should be outlawed. Since the old-time dyes (Ow! Jillian just pinched me for using "old-time"), as I was saying, some of the dyes used when Jillian and Kitty were kids have been banned and taken off the market. Anyway, I opted for a natural food coloring, along with using Total cereal, which is enriched with vitamins. The bad news? As you can see, that didn't work out so well in the color department. The good news? According to the judge's panel, they said they tasted just as good.

Tip for cleanup: Hot water will soak off residual marshmallow from the pan. So let some Christmas music rip and get in the holiday mood …

NOT-SO-GREEN HOLLY COOKIES

- ½ cup (equals 1 stick) of butter
- 32 large marshmallows (I used jet-puffed, campfire are good, too.)
- ½ teaspoon vanilla extract
- 1½ teaspoons of green food coloring (Use the traditional dye if you want them greener.)
- 3½ cups of Total cereal (or cornflakes)
- Cinnamon candies (in the aisle with the baking goods)

In a large, deep pan, melt butter first over medium heat. Add marshmallows and melt them with the butter, stirring constantly and mixing.

Add vanilla and food coloring, and stir to mix. Add cereal and stir until flakes are covered.

Scoop them out in small bunches onto GREASED waxed paper (use some cooking spray). Don't make the same mistake I did with one of the trays. Disaster. They stick like a... well, you get the picture.

Decorate each bunch with three candies each, press on so they stick. Let them cool and set. (I put them in the fridge for 15 minutes)

That's all there is to it. Sugary, marshmallowy fun.

So, this wraps it up for me. Hope to see you all back here on Happy Ever After again at some point. Until then, happy cooking. Thanks for all your support and readership, and for those of you who have enjoyed Jillian and my story in the *Caught Up in Raine Collection*, there's more of the McNally legacy coming with Jenny's and Kitty's stories. I've gotten an inside look, and you won't be disappointed. Jillian and I will be making guest appearances throughout. L.G. asked me to plug leaving a review if you've read any of the series.

Stay in touch. You can always find me in the Roost. Tweet me at @Raine's_Roost or drop by any time at www.lgoconnor.com.

A parting message from both Jillian and I: We wish you your

own happy ever after!

Happy Holidays to you and yours!

Peace out,
—Raine

Note to the Readers

Dear Readers,

Thank you so much for sharing *Recipes from Raine's Roost (aka Jillian's Kitchen)!*

If you haven't already, I hope you'll consider reading Jillian and Raine's story or other books in the Caught Up in Love series!

The Caught Up in Love series can be read as standalones, but reading them all gives you a few interlocking pieces that make the stories that much better. You will get further insight into all the central characters. The *Shelter My Heart* timeline starts during the second *Caught Up in RAINE* novelette, *Caught Up in Rachel.*

Before you go, please consider leaving a 1-2 sentence review on Amazon and Goodreads! For news on new releases as they happen, follow my author page on Amazon or join my newsletter on the next page for swag and exclusives.

Read on for an **exclusive chapter of *Caught Up in RAINE*!**

Hugs until next time!

~LG

Want more?

Sign up for the CAUGHT UP IN LOVE NEWSLETTER at www.lgoconnor.com for release updates and extras!

Get Caught Up again and again … in the **Caught Up in Love** series. Missed the full story? Catch Jillian and Raine's story from the beginning.

CAUGHT UP IN RAINE (Novel)
Two hearts. One soul-shattering decision. Experience Jillian and Raine's story as it evolves when a fortysomething romance writer plagued by loss comes to the rescue of a troubled twentysomething cover model.

REDISCOVERING RAINE (A Caught Up in Raine novelette)
Two hearts. One magical night. Pick up where we left off in CAUGHT UP IN RAINE, and experience Jillian and Raine's magical night after the bookstore. Putting a ring on Jillian's finger doesn't mean that all is easily forgiven.

CAUGHT UP IN RACHEL (A Caught Up in Raine novelette)
Two hearts. One small miracle. Be there as Jillian and Raine welcome Rachel into the world. Giving birth at an advanced maternal age isn't without peril, as Jillian discovers when she develops a condition that threatens mother and child.

SHELTER MY HEART (Novel)
Two weeks. One life-changing proposal. Engaged Jenny Lynch agrees to spend two weeks with Devon Soames, an ailing young CEO-in-training, who is due to inherit his dead father's conglomerate—if he can convince the board he's healthy and going to marry.

SURRENDER MY HEART (Novel)

Two old flames. One new destiny.

For decades, Katherine "Kitty" McNally has secretly loved John Henshaw, the man lying shot and unconscious in the hospital bed next to her. Then again, maybe not so secretly. Those closest to her, including her soon-to-be ex-husband, have suspected it for years. Their story ended with a gunshot wound the last time, too. Life seems to have taken her full circle, but only the dead know the secrets she still keeps.

Detective John Henshaw fell in love with his "Kat" the moment she became his geometry tutor in high school. When they graduated, he thought their future was sealed. Wrong. Enter life's nonstop curve balls. The worst two moments of his life were the two times he lost Kat. After thirty-five years and one failed marriage trying to forget her, he can't escape the fact that he's never stopped loving her. Maybe it's just his ego, but he could swear he sees a spark of love in her eyes every time she looks at him. It's why he stays in the New Jersey town that holds his most painful memories. It's why he accepted his place decades ago as a family friend to the McNally sisters.

As John recovers from his hospital stay in Kitty's care, they slowly rediscover each other. This is Kitty's last chance to confront her past and rekindle their love—if John can forgive her once he learns the truth.

Turn the page for a Caught Up in RAINE exclusive...

Caught Up in RAINE (Caught Up in Love #1)

Two Hearts.
One Soul-Shattering Decision.

A widow plagued by loss, fortysomething romance writer, Jillian Grant, comes to the rescue of a troubled twentysomething landscaper, Raine MacDonald, who bears an eerie resemblance to the male lead in her next novel. When Raine agrees to pose as her cover model, their chemistry ignites and Jillian must decide if age is more than just a number.

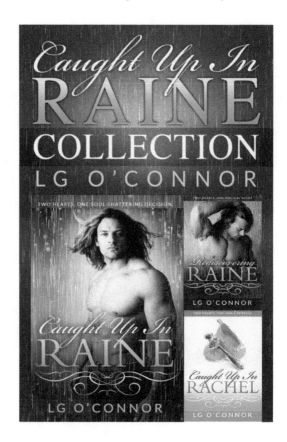

Excerpt—*Caught Up in RAINE*

JILLIAN

I glance at Raine in the rear view mirror as he follows me back to my house in his pickup. We stopped by the bar on the way home to pick up his wallet.

The doctor cleared him of any further head injuries and gave him enough painkillers for his ribs to last a couple of days. I popped up to see Vera quickly while Raine finished his appointment, but not before I shared my displeasure with the doctor about the hospital missing Raine's broken ribs in the first place. Vera was awake, and I was thrilled to see that she was doing even better. She was drifting off to sleep when I left. I almost feel optimistic.

I dial Kitty.

She picks up on the first ring. "Hey, Kitty. Don't kill me, but I need to cancel for later." I have a standing invitation every Sunday for dinner, a family tradition for as long as I can remember.

"Why? What's up?" my sister asks.

I take a deep breath and pray for minimal prying. "I have an unexpected house guest who's not feeling well."

"Who's staying with you?"

My jaw tightens. "A new friend. Someone with some cracked ribs."

"Jillian … Is it a man? I'm not sure I like the sound of this," she says with an unmistakable note of disapproval.

"Kitty, I'm old enough to make my own decisions. He's

not an axe murderer, so please stop mothering me."

"It's not that young gigolo Jenny told me about, that cover model, is it?" she says in a low voice.

My hackles rise. "I'm sorry, what did you say?"

"Jillian. I think you need to stick to men your own age. It's like you're dating someone who could be your child, for Heaven's sake!"

My face has to be beet-red because my cheeks are suddenly on fire. "I'm not dating him! He's just a friend. Why the hell am I justifying myself to you?" I channel Brigitte and lob over, "I can date or screw whomever I want as long as he's over the age of eighteen. I'll call you later." I disconnect my Bluetooth, wishing I had something to throw at someone. Instead, I slam my hand on the steering wheel. Other than making my palm sting, it barely takes the edge off. How dare she make me feel like a pedophile! And for her to insult him? What the hell was that about? A gigolo? Hardly. I consider myself a pretty good judge of character, and he hasn't given me that impression at all.

I pull into the garage and Raine pulls in front of the bay next to me, parking on the driveway. I make a mental note to dig up Robert's opener for him.

"What's the matter? You look pissed," he says as we walk into the kitchen from the garage.

I give him a wan smile. "My sister said something that did just that—pissed me off. I hung up on her."

His shoulders tense. "Jenny's mother?"

"She's the only sister I have. Why?"

He strolls over to the refrigerator and opens it. "I don't think Jenny likes me."

My eyes narrow at him. "Why do you say that?"

"Jillian, there's no food in here." He turns with a jar of mustard in his hand and arches his black-and-blue brow at me. "What do you do? Eat it on bread?"

I plant my hands on my hips. "Don't try to deflect my question. Why do you think Jenny doesn't like you?"

He straightens up and faces me, and then sweeps a hand over his bruised face. "She stopped me in the driveway after the photo shoot and shared her unflattering opinion of me. That I should stay away from you. What would someone like me possibly have to offer you beyond some eye candy to hang on your arm?" There's no mistaking the hurt and anger laced in his words.

My blood slowly boils as anger toward my family rises. He leans on the island with slumped shoulders. "I thought about staying away, not coming back. But I couldn't do it. I wanted to see you again. It's true, financially, right now, she's right. I don't have much to offer anyone. But I'm not interested in you because of your money, and hopefully the fact that I don't have any won't stop you. Money isn't everything. Of all people, I should know. Those other things she said? They're not true. That's not me at all."

He hangs his head, and asks quietly, "Do you want me to leave?"

My heart squeezes, and I want nothing more than to take away the layer of pain that seems to define him.

I walk around to meet him and pull him into my arms. "No. I definitely don't want you to leave." He wraps his arms tightly around me, rests his cheek on my hair, and lets out a deep breath. I melt into him, and the hard muscles of his chest feel good against me. His arms are strong and warm. I yearn to kiss him, and to comfort him—woman to man.

"Jillian?" he whispers.

"Yes?" I move my head from under his chin and look up. His eyes are glassy blue marbles as he gazes down at me. He swallows. "Thanks for believing me." I'm suddenly aware his lips are only inches from mine. My breath catches. A moment later, they come down and tenderly press to mine. He closes his eyes and the feel of his lips are soft yet firm. He squeezes me tighter in his arms, and his tongue parts my lips and enters my mouth, probing and caressing in the most gentle, sensuous dance. I follow his lead and relax into one of the finest kisses I ever remember experiencing. Raine's hands travel my back as his mouth becomes more insistent, and my body reacts with a rush of warmth and a clenching need. My hands find his hair and twist into the tawny softness of it. They meet in the back of his neck, and I pull him closer, mindful of his injuries.

He moans and I join him until we break away, breathless. My hands shake. I just kissed a man young enough to be … I stop myself from going there. Instead, I just admit that I loved it.

He rests his forehead next to mine. "Jillian …"

"Yes?"

"I'll be back."

"Huh?"

"There's no food in this house. Unless we both want to starve to death, I need to go to the store if I plan on cooking anything. My only other option is throwing you down on the kitchen floor and making love to you until I'm blind. But I'm thinking we need to start slower since I'll be staying here for a while, and I don't want to screw this up."

He releases me, and I stand there dumbstruck, rooted in place. His hand snatches his truck keys off the island and he heads for the door.

"Raine?" My head is swimming and I don't even know why I've called out his name. Only that I feel giddy, and I want confirmation that I didn't just imagine the last five minutes.

He turns. "Jillian?"

On impulse, as a display of trust, I rush to my purse, and take out the credit card I use just for groceries. "Here. You cook and I'll pay for the food. Deal?"

A slow smile comes to his lips. He takes the card and stuffs it into the pocket of his jeans. "Deal."

He turns to go.

"Raine?"

He spins on his heel. "Jillian, you're making me dizzy."

"Did you mean to kiss me?" I blurt.

A rakish smile forms on his lips like the one he used in the studio. "Yeah, and I plan on doing it again. Now let me go so I can get back and cook us a meal."

AVAILABLE NOW exclusively on Amazon!

Read FREE with Kindle Unlimited

Join the CAUGHT UP IN LOVE NEWSLETTER to find out about release schedules, pre-release copies, giveaways, and more!

About the Author

LG O'Connor is a corporate marketing exec by day who takes her author cape out at night. An avid reader, she loves books with memorable characters that make her heart sing. She's the author of the urban fantasy / paranormal romance series, *The Angelorum Twelve Chronicles*, and the romantic women's fiction series, *Caught Up in Love*, which debuted the award-winning novel, *Caught Up in RAINE*. The second book in the series, *Shelter My Heart*, was a 2017 Kindle Scout Winner. A native 'Jersey Girl,' she's always in search of the perfect cup of coffee and fine Italian leather. Her perfect hero always keeps the heroine fed. You can find recipes, which first appeared on USA Today's Happy Ever After blog, from the sexy hero of *Caught Up in RAINE* in his new cookbook, *Recipes from Raine's Roost aka Jillian's Kitchen*, available online where all fine books are sold.

CONTACT:

Website/Blog: www.lgoconnor.com

Facebook: www.Facebook.com/lgoconnor1

Twitter: twitter.com/lgoconnor1

Goodreads:www.goodreads.com/author/
show/7690970.L_G_O_Connor

Book Site: www.caughtupinraine.com

Email: lg@lgoconnor.com

Other Books

TRINITY STONES, Book One in the *Angelorum Twelve Chronicles* series is available now where all fine books are sold.

"O'Connor tackles important world building, while also kicking off the story with a bang." ~**Publisher's Weekly**

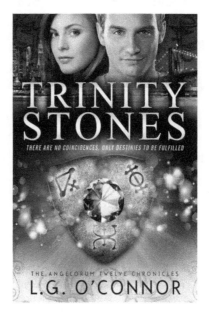

On her 27th birthday, Cara Collins, a single New York investment banker with an anxiety disorder, receives a stunning inheritance and is taken under the wing of angels. When Dr. Kai Solomon, Cara's longtime friend and first love, is kidnapped by dark force, Cara must choose: accept her place in a 2,000-year-old prophecy foretold in the Trinity Stones as the First of the Holy Twelve who will lead the final battle between good and evil ... or risk losing everything she holds dear.

Genre: Paranormal: Angels / Urban Fantasy / Paranormal Romance
Audience: Ages 18+ / adult language and content
Publisher: She Writes Press
ISBN-13: 978-1-938314-84-1 (Trade Paperback)
ISBN-13: 978-1-938314-85-8 (eBook)

WANDERER'S CHILDREN, Book Two in the *Angelorum Twelve Chronicles* series is available where all fine books are sold.

"Combining a marvelous talent for emotional resonance with a naturally light, playful attitude towards sex and romance, L.G. O'Connor creates a rich, complex world that realistically explores joy, pain, fame, child abuse, and the insanely complex and frightening realities of pre-established hierarchies. Although set in a supernatural milieu, the emotions and situations these characters find themselves in ring with a clarity that is unforgettable. **THE WANDERER'S CHILDREN** (4.5 stars) is a satisfying and nuanced read for fans of the series and newbies alike." ~**IndieReader**

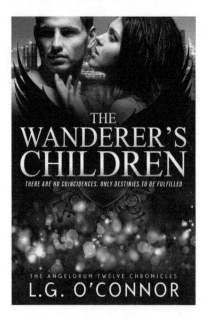

Cara's second chance encounter with rock star Brett King is no coincidence. One of the Wanderer's Children, he and the blood of his secret siblings are the key to gathering the rest of the Twelve ... if betrayal and Lucifer don't rip them apart first.

Genre: Paranormal: Angels / Urban Fantasy / Paranormal Romance
Audience: Ages 18+ / adult language and content
Publisher: Collins-Young Publishing
ISBN-13: 978-0-990738-10-7 (Trade Paperback)
ISBN-13: 978-0-990738-14-5 (eBook)

HOPE'S PRELUDE, Book 2.5 in the *Angelorum Twelve Chronicles.* See where it all begins…

For fans of the series or those tipping their toe into the World of Angelorum for the first time, this prequel novella gives us a glimpse into what happens to shape destiny before *Trinity Stones* begins and hints at what will happen next in the series.

"A unique twist of the angels vs. demons mythology that blends science with religion and includes characters that grab you by the heart!"—**Maria V. Snyder, New York Times Bestselling Author**

While dealing with visions of her death, Dr. Sandra Wilson races against the clock to develop a genetic vaccine that will, in the future, save the life of the one who will lead the final battle between angels and demons.

Enter the world of the Angelorum, and get a view into the genetics project that started it all as destinies entwine to deliver us one step closer to battle. There are no coincidences...

Genre: Paranormal: Angels / Urban Fantasy / Romance
Audience: Appropriate for readers of both the adult and young adult versions of the series
Publisher: Collins-Young Publishing
ISBN-13: 978-0-990738-17-6 (Trade Paperback)
ISBN-13: 978-0-990738-16-9 (eBook)

COMING NEXT in *The Angelorum Twelve Chronicles:*

BOOK of FOUR RINGS, Book 3, SPRING 2018

Series conclusion, **WELL of SOULS,** Book 4, WINTER 2019

CPSIA information can be obtained
at www.ICGtesting.com
Printed in the USA
LVHW06s0620090818
586460LV00009B/24/P

9 780997 062373